SPIRIT

Illustrations by Josephine Wall

This is a FLAME TREE Book

FLAME TREE PUBLISHING
6 Melbray Mews, Fulham,
London SW6 3NS, United Kingdom
www.flametreepublishing.com

First published 2019

19 21 23 22 20
1 3 5 7 9 10 8 6 4 2

ISBN: 978-1-78755-687-4

The cover image features *Wings*
by Josephine Wall

© Josephine Wall 2019

A copy of the CIP data for this book is available from the British
Library.

Printed and bound in China

SPIRIT

Illustrations by Josephine Wall

THOUGHTS TO INSPIRE & MOTIVATE

FLAME TREE
PUBLISHING

SPIRIT

Illustrations by Josephine Wall

Spirit: Thoughts, Quotes and Poetry

6–87

Artist at Work: Josephine Wall

An insight into the working methods, influences
and studio of a remarkable artist.

88–95

Gaia, the Greek
Goddess, is Mother
Earth, the bringer
of life and beauty.
Josephine Wall

My dreams were all my own; I accounted for them to nobody; they were my refuge when annoyed – my dearest pleasure when free.

Mary Shelley

No pessimist ever discovered
the secrets of the stars, or
sailed to an uncharted land,
or opened a new heaven to
the human spirit.

Hellen Keller

When you daydream, all things are possible. You can fly like the wind on a unicorn, across a magical plain strewn with flowers and a million stars.

Josephine Wall

Spirit is the real and eternal; matter is the unreal and temporal.

Mary Baker-Eddy

Composing gives me
great pleasure ... There is
nothing which surpasses
the joy of creation, if
only because through it
one wins hours of self-
forgetfulness, when one
lives in a world of sound.
Clara Schumann

The mellifluous voice of the Goddess welcomes her to this enchanted land, with colourful trees and flowers. A pathway to a land, which seems full of colour and light, compared with the grey cold world through which she has travelled.

Josephine Wall

As a new dawn approaches
Gaia emerges from our
sleeping planet. The
radiance of her aura lights
up the heavens and her
'presence' gives confidence
to the birds and animals
to venture forth, secure in
the knowledge that she will
protect them.

Josephine Wall

Raging seas challenge
our courage to the limits,
teaching us the skills and
strength we will need to
endure the storms and
darkness ahead.

Josephine Wall

I longed to arrest all beauty that came before me, and at length the longing has been satisfied.

Julia Margaret Cameron

Mortals hold seashells
to their ears to hear the
sounds of the seas and
imagine life in the deep
waters below. Perhaps a
mermaid would look into
a seashell to see and hear
the sights and sounds of
the Earth above.

Josephine Wall

You can't use up creativity.
The more you use, the
more you have.

Maya Angelou

Andromeda sails away
in her magical galleon
in search of adventure
beyond earthly
boundaries to worlds
beyond the stars.

Josephine Wall

The great enemy of creativity
is fear. When we're fearful,
we freeze up – like a nine-
year-old who won't draw
pictures, for fear everybody
will laugh. Creativity has a
lot to do with a willingness
to take risks.

Faith Ringgold

The spirit, I think, is a stream, a fountain, and must be continually poured out, for only if it is poured out will more and clearer streams come.

Brenda Ueland

Those who contemplate
the beauty of the Earth find
reserves of strength that will
endure as long as life lasts.

Rachel Carson

As you enter positions of trust and power, dream a little before you think.

Toni Morrison

The captured butterflies come alive and unfurl their colourful wings as they escape into the waiting world, whirling around in celebration of their newfound freedom.

Josephine Wall

There is nothing so
beautiful as the free forest.
To catch a fish when you are
hungry, cut the boughs of
a tree, make fire to roast it,
and eat it in the open air, is
the greatest of all luxuries. I
would not stay a week pent
up in cities, if it were not for
my passion for Art.

Edmonia Lewis

Love is like a
mysterious ship
that can carry us
on a voyage of the
imagination.

Josephine Wall

You know I am not born to tread in the beaten track – the peculiar bent of my nature pushes me on.

Mary Wollstonecraft

We reap what we sow, but nature has love over and above that justice, and gives us shadow and blossom and fruit, that spring from no planting of ours.

George Eliot
(Scenes of Clerical Life)

No circumstances can ever make or mar the unfolding of the spiritual life. Spirituality does not depend upon the environment; it depends upon one's attitude towards life.

Annie Besant

I'll walk where my own nature would be leading:
It vexes me to choose another guide.

Emily Brontë
(Often Rebuked)

44

Beneath her multicoloured, gossamer headdress beats the heart of a lion offering strength to the gentle souls in flight.

Josephine Wall

The soul is a breath of
living spirit, that with
excellent sensitivity,
permeates the entire body
to give it life. Just so, the
breath of the air makes the
Earth fruitful. Thus the air
is the soul of the Earth,
moistening it, greening it.

Hildegard of Bingen

Several worlds meet in this union of the Earth, sea and sky. Confusing to some, but perfectly accepted by a child.

Josephine Wall

There are some things you learn best in calm, and some in storm.

Willa Cather

(The Song of the Lark)

Nearly hidden by nettles, wild briar and foxgloves did I espy a fleeting glimpse of gossamer wing? Was there a little face with a special 'look'? Was the 'look' surprise, or could it be a secret smile?

Josephine Wall

Every mystery solved
brings us to the threshold
of a greater one.
Rachel Carson

You only have what you give.
It's by spending yourself
that you become rich.

Isabel Allende

There are many paths to follow and many doors to open (if you choose) which lead to different directions in life. Is it just a game of chance – the mere roll of a dice or is everything pre-ordained – a path laid out just for you?

Josephine Wall

Everybody is two beings:
one lives in the daylight
and stands guard. The
other being walks and
howls at night.

Zora Neale Hurston

(Moses, Man of the Mountain)

We're all capable of
climbing so much higher
than we usually permit
ourselves to suppose.

Octavia E. Butler

There is a solitude
of space
A solitude of sea
A solitude of death,
but these
Society shall be
Compared with that
profounder site
That polar privacy
A soul admitted to itself.
– Finite infinity.

Emily Dickinson

The mind is like a richly
woven tapestry in which the
colors are distilled from the
experiences of the senses,
and the design drawn
from the convolutions
of the intellect.

Carson McCullers
(Reflections in a Golden Eye)

In the garden of our
hearts, where memories
grow, warm thoughts
unfold and bring us cheer,
like bright pansy blossoms,
sunny and sweet, as we
fondly remember those
we hold dear.

Josephine Wall

If one is lucky a solitary
fantasy can totally
transform one million
realities.

Maya Angelou
(The Heart of a Woman)

I am I and Earth is Earth –
mesa, sky, wind, rushing
river. Each is an entity but
the essence of the Earth
flows into me – perhaps of
me into the Earth.
Edith Warner

Those who never sink into this peace of nature lose a tremendous well of strength, for there is something healing and life-giving in the mere atmosphere surrounding a country house.

Eleanor Roosevelt

As she drifts into a trance like state, she imagines herself adorned with peacocks and exotic flowers. She enjoys her fleeting moments of escapism.

Josephine Wall

Who can say which is the greater sign of creative power, the Sun with its planet system swinging with governed impetus to some incalculable end, or the gold sallow catkin with its flashing system of little flies?

Mary Webb

She quietly expected great
things to happen to her,
and no doubt that's one of
the reasons why they did.

Zelda Fitzgerald

Inner space is
the real frontier.
Gloria Steinem

I am sure there is Magic in everything, only we have not sense enough to get hold of it and make it do things for us...

Frances Hodgson Burnett
(The Secret Garden)

After her dancing is done,

the wind carries her home

on a playful breeze. Each

miracle of nature's beauty

fills her heart with joy.

Josephine Wall

Their thoughts and
pulses race as the
heavenly conductor
leads them to a
crescendo in the
concerto of love.
The enchantment
of that moment will
last forever.
Josephine Wall

So what is wild? What is wilderness? What are dreams but an internal wilderness and what is desire but a wildness of the soul?

Louise Erdrich

Artist at Work: Josephine Wall

Josephine Wall's fantasy art is the work of an extraordinary imagination writ large, at once otherworldly yet celebrating the world we inhabit and the spirit of our inner selves. Her magical scenes, full of vivid colours and light, cannot help but inspire warmth and joy – not to mention all of the captivating, intricate details that invite the viewer to delve into the enchanted realm she has created.

A prolific and industrious artist, painting is just one of Josephine's many creative outlets: 'I enjoy many creative pursuits including sculpture, pottery, decorating my own clothes and boots, and making topiary bushes in the garden.' Her passion for art and visual storytelling goes back to her childhood:

'I became interested in painting because from the age of three my dad would draw images for my amusement. The images would appear as if by magic – entrancing me. I was obsessed, and my course was set for life.' It is Josephine's steadfast love of 'creating in any form' that has remained the driving force of motivation throughout her career as an artist: 'I feel so lucky to have this gift which I have enjoyed all my life, and be able to share it with others around the world.'

In the Studio

Josephine's attic studio, featuring a pyramid-shaped roof and walls decorated with hand-painted wisteria, is the perfect environment to kindle inspiration as her work takes shape. Josephine describes her creative process as a fluid one, and that she is 'often surprised at the finished piece.'

The painting 'usually starts with an idea which evolves as it develops... I only do a rough sketch at the beginning because as the painting evolves it can change many times.'

Working from a prized mahogany and brass easel Josephine once purchased with her father at auction years ago, each painting takes roughly three to four weeks to complete, depending on the scale. Her preferred medium is Daler Rowney Cryla acrylic paint, as, 'it dries fast, does not oxidise, yellow or crack, and I can use it to produce thick textured areas or diluted for washes or detail.' Another way Josephine produces texture in her paintings is by using a palette knife to create a 'veiny' effect for tree bark, leaves and fairy wings. Josephine says she knows that a painting is almost finished when she starts to add 'hidden faces', one of her enchanting signature details.

Influences

The work of Surrealist artists such as Salvador Dali, Greek mythology and the literature of J.R.R. Tolkien are just some of Josephine's sources of inspiration. She also cites the influence of 'the romanticism of the Pre-Raphaelites, the drawings of Arthur Rackham (especially his trees), and the Art Nouveau of Alphonse Mucha', and praises the work of Kinuko Craft and Mahmoud Farshchian, as well as other fantasy artists. Based in Dorset, her work is equally informed by her environment: 'We live in a lovely area – close to the sea, New Forest, and the Purbeck Hills, all of which are a great source of inspiration.' The beauty of nature and the changing seasons are an ever-present theme in Josephine's work, and her home is an ideal vantage point from which to observe them firsthand.

Looking Ahead

While Josephine's paintings are largely fantasy, the sentiment behind much of her work is grounded in reality, particularly with regards to the importance of the natural world and the future of our planet. Josephine takes the platform she has as an artist seriously: 'Artists have been given a fabulous gift, but with it come great responsibilities. We have the chance to change the world by portraying images of how life could be and how it should be.' In particular, Josephine's Gaia paintings emphasise the dangers of pollution and de-forestation, and the importance of conservation. Through these paintings, she hopes to motivate mankind to 'do everything possible to protect our precious and beautiful planet, and heal the damage we have already inflicted.' Beautiful as well as inspiring, the art of Josephine Wall will surely continue to resonate with viewers everywhere.

THOUGHTS TO INSPIRE & MOTIVATE